CAROLINE BIRD

Caroline Bird is a poet and playwright. She has had eight volumes of poetry published by Carcanet, including *In These Days of Prohibition* (2017), which was shortlisted for the T. S. Eliot Prize and the Ted Hughes Award, *The Air Year* (2020), which won The Forward Prize for Best Collection 2020 and was shortlisted for the Costa Prize and the Polari Prize, and her selected poems *Rookie* (2022) and *Ambush at Still Lake* (2024). She won a Cholmondeley Award in 2023, for sustained excellence across a body of work.

Caroline began writing plays as a teenager and was a member of the Royal Court Young Writers' Programme. She has been shortlisted for the Susan Smith Blackburn Prize, and as Most Promising New Playwright at the Off West End Theatre Awards. Her plays include *The Trojan Women* (Gate Theatre); *Chamber Piece* (Lyric Theatre Hammersmith); *The Wonderful Wizard of Oz* (Northern Stage) and *Red Ellen* (Northern Stage/Nottingham Playhouse/Royal Lyceum Edinburgh), which was shortlisted for the 2021 George Devine Award, recognising new writing and powerful voices.

Other Titles in this Series

Waleed Akhtar
THE ART OF ILLUSION *after* Alexis Michalik
KABUL GOES POP: MUSIC TELEVISION
    AFGHANISTAN
THE P WORD
THE REAL ONES

Caroline Bird
RED ELLEN

Chris Bush
THE ASSASSINATION OF KATIE HOPKINS
    with Matt Winkworth
THE CHANGING ROOM
CHRIS BUSH PLAYS: ONE
A DOLL'S HOUSE *after* Ibsen
FAUSTUS: THAT DAMNED WOMAN
HUNGRY
JANE EYRE *after* Brontë
THE LAST NOËL
OTHERLAND
ROBIN HOOD AND THE
    CHRISTMAS HEIST
    with Matt Winkworth
ROCK / PAPER / SCISSORS
STANDING AT THE SKY'S EDGE
    with Richard Hawley
STEEL

Jez Butterworth
THE FERRYMAN
THE HILLS OF CALIFORNIA
JERUSALEM
JEZ BUTTERWORTH PLAYS: ONE
JEZ BUTTERWORTH PLAYS: TWO
MOJO
THE NIGHT HERON
PARLOUR SONG
THE RIVER
THE WINTERLING

Caryl Churchill
BLUE HEART
CHURCHILL PLAYS: THREE
CHURCHILL PLAYS: FOUR
CHURCHILL PLAYS: FIVE
CHURCHILL: SHORTS
CLOUD NINE
DING DONG THE WICKED
A DREAM PLAY *after* Strindberg
DRUNK ENOUGH TO SAY I LOVE YOU?
ESCAPED ALONE
FAR AWAY
GLASS. KILL. BLUEBEARD'S FRIENDS.
    IMP.
HERE WE GO
HOTEL
ICECREAM
LIGHT SHINING IN BUCKINGHAMSHIRE
LOVE AND INFORMATION
MAD FOREST
A NUMBER
PIGS AND DOGS
SEVEN JEWISH CHILDREN
THE SKRIKER
THIS IS A CHAIR
THYESTES *after* Seneca
TRAPS
WHAT IF IF ONLY

Lucy Kirkwood
BEAUTY AND THE BEAST
    with Katie Mitchell
BLOODY WIMMIN
THE CHILDREN
CHIMERICA
HEDDA *after* Ibsen
THE HUMAN BODY
IT FELT EMPTY WHEN THE HEART
    WENT AT FIRST BUT IT IS
    ALRIGHT NOW
LUCY KIRKWOOD PLAYS: ONE
MOSQUITOES
NSFW
RAPTURE
TINDERBOX
THE WELKIN

Winsome Pinnock
LEAVE TAKING
PIG HEART BOY *after* Malorie Blackman
ROCKETS AND BLUE LIGHTS
TAKEN
TITUBA

Stef Smith
ENOUGH
GIRL IN THE MACHINE
HUMAN ANIMALS
NORA : A DOLL'S HOUSE
REMOTE
SWALLOW

Jack Thorne
2ND MAY 1997
AFTER LIFE *after* Hirokazu Kore-eda
BUNNY
BURYING YOUR BROTHER IN
    THE PAVEMENT
A CHRISTMAS CAROL *after* Dickens
THE END OF HISTORY…
HOPE
JACK THORNE PLAYS: ONE
JACK THORNE PLAYS: TWO
JUNKYARD
LET THE RIGHT ONE IN
    after John Ajvide Lindqvist
THE MOTIVE AND THE CUE
MYDIDAE
THE SOLID LIFE OF SUGAR WATER
STACY & FANNY AND FAGGOT
WHEN WINSTON WENT TO WAR WITH
    THE WIRELESS
WHEN YOU CURE ME
WOYZECK *after* Büchner

debbie tucker green
BORN BAD
DEBBIE TUCKER GREEN PLAYS: ONE
DIRTY BUTTERFLY
EAR FOR EYE
HANG
NUT
A PROFOUNDLY AFFECTIONATE,
    PASSIONATE DEVOTION TO
    SOMEONE (– *NOUN*)
RANDOM
STONING MARY
TRADE & GENERATIONS
TRUTH AND RECONCILIATION

Caroline Bird

THE LAST STAND OF MRS. MARY WHITEHOUSE

NICK HERN BOOKS
London
www.nickhernbooks.co.uk

A Nick Hern Book

The Last Stand of Mrs. Mary Whitehouse first published in Great Britain in 2025 as a paperback original by Nick Hern Books Limited, The Glasshouse, 49a Goldhawk Road, London W12 8QP

The Last Stand of Mrs. Mary Whitehouse copyright © 2025 Caroline Bird

Caroline Bird has asserted her right to be identified as the author of this work

Front cover: photograph of Maxine Peake by Craig Fleming; photograph of Mary Whitehouse by Patrick McGuiness/Shutterstock; design by Feast Creative

Designed and typeset by Nick Hern Books, London
Printed in Great Britain by Mimeo Ltd, Huntingdon, Cambridgeshire PE29 6XX

A CIP catalogue record for this book is available from the British Library

ISBN 978 1 83904 491 5

CAUTION All rights whatsoever in this play are strictly reserved. Requests to reproduce the text in whole or in part should be addressed to the publisher. This book may not be used, in whole or in part, for the development or training of artificial intelligence technologies or systems.

Amateur Performing Rights Applications for performance, including readings and excerpts, by amateurs in the English language throughout the world should be addressed to the Performing Rights Manager, Nick Hern Books, The Glasshouse, 49a Goldhawk Road, London W12 8QP, *tel* +44 (0)20 8749 4953, *email* rights@nickhernbooks.co.uk, except as follows:

Australia: ORiGiN Theatrical, *email* enquiries@originmusic.com.au, *web* www.origintheatrical.com.au

New Zealand: Play Bureau, 20 Rua Street, Mangapapa, Gisborne, 4010, *tel* +64 21 258 3998, *email* info@playbureau.com

United States of America and Canada: The Agency (London) Ltd, see details below

Professional Performing Rights Applications for performance by professionals in any medium and in any language throughout the world (and amateur and stock performances in the United States of America and Canada) should be addressed to The Agency (London) Ltd, 24 Pottery Lane, Holland Park, London W11 4LZ, *fax* +44 (0)20 7727 9037, *email* info@theagency.co.uk

No performance of any kind may be given unless a licence has been obtained. Applications should be made before rehearsals begin. Publication of this play does not necessarily indicate its availability for amateur performance.

www.nickhernbooks.co.uk/environmental-policy

Nick Hern Books' authorised representative in the EU is
Easy Access System Europe – Mustamäe tee 50, 10621 Tallinn, Estonia
email gpsr.requests@easproject.com

The Last Stand of Mrs. Mary Whitehouse was first performed at Nottingham Playhouse on 5 September 2025, with the following cast:

MARY WHITEHOUSE	Maxine Peake
EVERYONE ELSE	Samuel Barnett
Director	Sarah Frankcom
Designer	Peter Butler
Lighting Designer	Malcolm Rippeth
Sound Designer & Composer	Annie May Fletcher
Movement Director	Jennifer Jackson
Voice & Dialect Coach	Liz Flint
Wigs, Hair & Makeup	Helen Keane for Campbell Young Associates
Company Stage Manager	Patricia Davenport
Deputy Stage Manager	Sarah Longson
Assistant Stage Manager	Daisy Vahey
Head of Construction	Janine Forster
Head of Costume	Emilie Carter
Dresser	Lucy Edgeworth
Wigs & Dresser	Eloisa Roan
Apprentice Costume Technician	Rachel Tooley
Costume Maker	Jules Sheppard
Costume Maker	Charlotte Elliot
Costume Maker	Lauren Allsopp
Head of Lighting & Video	Molly Stammers
Deputy Head of Lighting & Video	Ryan Moore
Lighting Technician	Penny Coke-Woods
Director of Producing	Amanda Bruce
Trainee Producer	Leila Glen
Head of Production	Andrew Quick
Technical & Production Manager	Jamie Smith
Head of Props	Hannah Zemlak
Props Assistant	Hannah Boothman

Head of Scenic Art	Claire Thompson
Scenic Artist	Erin Fleming
Scenic Artist	Anna Roberts
Head of Sound	Matt Sims
Deputy Head of Sound	Tom Codd
Sound Technician	Cameron Lloyd
Head of Stage	Tony Topping
Deputy Head of Stage	Kushal Patel
Stage Technician	Laura Wolczyk
Stage Technician	James van Aardt
Apprentice Technician	Jace Daws
Apprentice Technician	Dylan Evans

Sets, Scenic Art, Costume, Props, Lighting, Sound, Video, Stage Management and Technical are made or managed by the Nottingham Playhouse team, supported by freelancers.

Piccalilli

The Nottingham Playhouse run of this production was sponsored by Piccalilli.

Acknowledgments

Thanks to Sarah Frankcom for her pin-sharp dramaturgical guidance, wisdom and advice throughout the drafting process.

Thanks to Adam Penford for having the idea for a Mary Whitehouse play and for believing in the project from the beginning.

Thanks to Eleanor Lloyd and Kate Pakenham for their feedback and support.

Thanks to Maxine Peake and Samuel Barnett for being the best cast a writer could hope for.

Thanks to the entire creative team and everyone at Nottingham Playhouse.

Thanks to my agent, Emily Hickman.

And thanks, as always, to my wonderful wife, Eliza – I love you.

C.B.

Characters

MARY WHITEHOUSE
DAVID, *a young documentary film-maker*
JACOB, *a student*
RICHARD, *a youth counsellor*
HENRY, *a friend of Young Mary*
ADAM, *a vicar*
JOSEPH, *a nurse in a care home*
CECILIA, *mother of Maria, a lesbian student at Oxford*
JOHN SMYTH, *barrister and Christian conservative*
DENIS LEMON, *editor of* Gay News
GEOFFREY ROBERTSON, *barrister and human rights lawyer*
BEATRICE HUTCHESON, *Mary's mother*
MARGARET THATCHER
JILL TWEEDIE, *a feminist journalist from the* Guardian
A ROMAN CENTURION
ANONYMOUS PHONE CALLERS
PROTESTERS
FOREMAN
COURT CLERK
JUDGE
SOFT-SPOKEN BRISTOLIAN WOMAN
CONFIDENT YOUNG WELSHMAN
ELDERLY WOMAN FROM THE EAST END
YOUNG YORKSHIRE MAN WITH SLIGHT LISP
OLD IRISH MAN
TV CONTINUITY ANNOUNCER
ERNEST WHITEHOUSE
NURSE
JESUS

Actor One plays Mary Whitehouse (including Young Mary).
Actor Two plays everyone else.

The scenes are numbered (in twenty-eight sections) to make it clearer to read, but each scene overlaps/flows into the next.

Note on Play

This play is a work of fiction inspired by real events. Some characters and scenes have been imagined, or conflated from various sources including diaries, court records and interviews.

This text went to press before the end of rehearsals and so may differ slightly from the play as performed.

1

The curtains are closed.

As the house lights are going down, MARY WHITEHOUSE *peeks through the curtains at the audience.*

MARY. If I stay in here with the curtains drawn for an hour, eventually they'll get bored and go away.

It's what they want, of course. To shame me into isolation.

Matthew Fifteen, do not light a lamp and put it under a basket, but on a lampstand... that they may *see* your good works. Yes.

I'm getting dressed.

Colour, as much as possible.

If they're expecting some dowdy busybody, they've got another thing coming.

It's a glorious summer's day.

I am coming out.

MARY *opens the curtains, glorious, triumphant.*

We are in Mary's garden.
August 1977.
Summerhouse, lawn chairs, tea trolley, garden hose, flowers, etc. A folding table with a telephone, a Bible, a notebook, piles of letters and binoculars.

Cass Elliot's 'Make Your Own Kind of Music' plays on the radio.

Ernest, switch it off.

Music stops.

PROTESTERS. Buggery is beautiful! Buggery is beautiful! Buggery is beautiful!

MARY (*to the audience*). There used to be nothing odd about us.
Do you remember?
We all seemed to have one child after another.
They all used to play in the garden
with the sand and the water.
We were all of the same mind.

Now our house is surrounded by gays.

It's usually very quiet here, with our chickens, geese and
fantail pigeons on the fringe of Constable Country,
surrounded by our meadow. That makes me sound very
grand. I should say, surrounded by this rough-looking acre of
land I euphemistically call our meadow…

and they're just on the other side
past the greenhouse
in a great big line
staring at me
with their megaphones and placards,
wishing me dead.

I wish them well.

(*Looking through binoculars*.) 'Mary Whitehouse Kills.'
Kills who? Who have I killed?

Phone rings.

Hello, Ardleigh two-one-four-five, this is Mrs Mary
Whitehouse speaking.

ANONYMOUS CALLER 1. This is just to let you know, your assassination is still on.

MARY. I beg your pardon?

ANONYMOUS CALLER 1. If the appeal is won, we're still going to get you.

They hang up.

MARY. Hello?

She puts the phone down.

Death threats. Against a sixty-seven-year-old woman. And they call *me* hateful?

(*Referring to a pile of letters.*) I also get charming letters. (*Unfolding one.*) Me with a meat cleaver in my back. Courtesy of 'the oppressed minority'.

(*Looking through binoculars.*)
Bearded man in tiny waistcoat with no shirt underneath.
Long-haired waif in tight white T-shirt.
Almost-bald woman in leather jacket.
Denim man with his arms crossed.
Mad-hatter type with a sign saying 'Sissies Unite'.

There's no neighbours over there, it's a public footpath but it's very secluded.
This protest is all for *my* benefit.

An ordinary Christian who collects pebbles for a hobby.

I've got tottering piles scattered all round the house,
don't ask why, it's probably
the most interesting thing about me
and even that is completely unremarkable.

Phone rings.

Hello, Ardleigh two-one-four-five, this is Mrs Mary Whitehouse speaking.

ANONYMOUS CALLER 2. I want to tell you, Mrs Whitehouse, that I am a homosexual and I'm glad that I'm a homosexual.

MARY. Well, if it makes you feel better to have told me, I'm delighted, thank you very much for calling, goodbye.

She hangs up.

(*To the audience.*) He doesn't sound very glad.

2

Enter DAVID (*the documentary film-maker*). *He's just had an egg thrown in his face.*

DAVID. They're holding my soundman hostage.

MARY. David, your face!

DAVID. I thought I'd spare my soft-top by parking up in the village, but when we refused to film them, they turned vicious. Last time I saw Marcus, he was being screamed at by a bloke in a floral headdress. It's a miracle I saved our equipment. (*Using the hose to rinse his hair.*) It used to be the love that dare not speak its name, now you can't bloody shut it up! Pardon my French.

MARY. Oh, you can't use the garden hose, I'll get you a damp cloth –

DAVID. It's just an egg, and time is of the essence.

MARY. The egg-sense.

DAVID (*drying his face with his shirt*). You are hilarious. I want our film to show *this* side of you as well.

Little beat.

Are you alright, Mrs Whitehouse?

MARY. Yes. Let's get some natural shots first: pruning the roses, reading my Bible –

DAVID. 'Cause if these little bastards – pardon my French – were comparing *me* to Hitler, I'd be sobbing myself to sleep.

MARY. I'm not a crier.

DAVID. No shame in it.

MARY. Truly. (*As if this is just occurring to her.*) I can't remember the last time I cried.

MARY *poses with her Bible, ready to be filmed.*

Right.

DAVID (*struggling with the equipment*). One sec. Dick Van Dyke with his one-man band over here. Granada only pays half my petrol. If I were the BBC, you'd have a whole camera crew of pinko lefties trampling your lawn.

MARY. Perhaps these rival channels will make the BBC remember their values. Before 'family television' became giant pepper pots with phallic guns.

DAVID. Exterminate! Exterminate!

MARY. It's not a joke, David. Shootings, electrocutions, drownings, torture. Young minds are like wet cement. Our licensing fees are funding children's nightmares.

DAVID. And yours too, watching all that.

MARY. Oh, I don't watch it all. Tireless volunteers send me monitoring reports. I'd fear for my soul, consuming every writhe and curse, every spurt of blood. (*Shudders*.) Absolutely not!

MARY *picks up the phone and dials a number.*

Terry? It's Mrs Whitehouse. The rainbow coach has arrived and I can't see your reporter.

Pause, listening.

I hope he's on his way. Or next time, I'll ring the *Mail*. Best regards to your wife.

She hangs up.

(*To* DAVID.) Film me bringing out the cake.

DAVID. Action.

DAVID *films as* MARY *wheels out a pre-prepared trolley.*

Cut.

He stops filming.

Victoria sponge, my favourite, with fresh raspberries –

MARY. From the garden.

DAVID. And what beautiful doilies. (*Holding one up to the light*.) Like a snowflake.

MARY *observes him.*

MARY. Do you have a girlfriend, David?

DAVID. Why, you interested?

MARY (*ignoring his joke*). No wedding ring but I assume you're courting? Handsome man like you.

DAVID. Ha. Shall we do the interview in the conservatory?

MARY. Please answer my question first.

MARY *smiles at him.*

DAVID. Why are you asking me this now?

MARY. I want to understand why you are working with me, David.

DAVID. It's my shoulders, isn't it? I've got weak shoulders.

MARY *smiles at him.*

Because I'm a grown-up, not a fantasist, that's why. This lot, they're like shoplifters shouting 'justice for shoplifters'; they'd rather change the moral framework of the world than change themselves. Not me. Yes, I struggle. But I do know right from wrong. My father's a vicar and he's just like you, Mrs Whitehouse, and I thought maybe he might watch our documentary and see that… that… I am nothing like… I am certainly not proud.

MARY *appears satisfied with this answer.*

MARY. Right. Just the peach turtleneck or with the blue cardigan?

DAVID (*wiping his eyes*). Blue. Brings out your eyes.

MARY. Fire away.

After he recovers, DAVID *starts filming. In lieu of a soundman, he sets the camera rolling and then picks up the boom.*

DAVID. Rolling. (*Claps*.) The first trial for blasphemy in fifty-six years was held this summer in London. It seemed to many an eccentric event but it raised a vital question: can any belief still be held so sacred that it should be protected by law? Campaigner Mary Whitehouse, who began the prosecution, often protests about horror movies, rock songs and pornography, but did she ever imagine her greatest public battle to date would centre around, not a B-movie blood-fest, but a single poem published last year in *Gay News*?

MARY. I write poems. When my children were small, I wrote many – not very good – poems whilst they played in the garden or on the beach. This poem, however, is an abomination against God.

DAVID. Could you describe it?

MARY. It seeks to violate the very core of our natures, undo the bonds that hold communities together and pervert the collective mind. I shan't say more than that.

DAVID. The poet, James Kirkup, a professor of literature, was not on trial. Instead, Mrs Whitehouse lodged her complaint against the newspaper itself, and its editor, Denis Lemon. Why not prosecute the poet?

MARY. Well, he's clearly mentally ill. Must be, to have written that. No, I felt it kinder to hold the publication responsible.

DAVID. Because your detractors have accused you of using this trial as a means to an end...?

MARY. What end?

DAVID. A long-held desire to shut down *Gay News*?

MARY. Do I look like I sit in my armchair, with my cup of tea, scanning 'gay' newspapers, waiting for something sufficiently litigious?

DAVID. No, Mrs Whitehouse, you certainly don't.

MARY. If this thing had been published in the *Catholic Herald*, I'd have prosecuted *them* for blasphemy. (*Laughing*.) This

trial was not about homosexuality. It was about the rights of
Christians not to have our feelings offended, but that right
has been almost completely submerged by the rights of
homosexuals not to have *their* feelings offended! I'm sorry
but *everything* is not *always* about *their* feelings.

DAVID. Cut.

MARY. How did that sound?

DAVID. Like the voice of reason.

3

MARY (*to the audience*).
  It was the summer of the ladybirds. 1976.
  Thousands filling the air, carpeting the ground,
  swarms and swarms
  and I was out here, my arms, my face covered in ladybirds,
  I was mostly ladybird, just overwhelmed, enveloped
  in God's creatures, tiny, identical, beautiful,
  all working for the same purpose,
  filling the earth and the sky. A majority!
  And I looked up, and I spoke directly to God and I said,
  Alright, I see, something's going to happen this year.
  This is the year that the little people
  will lift their voices once again to be heard
  and sure enough
  when the weather turned, and the swarm
  – the sign – subsided, plop,
  a letter landed on the mat.

  The morning had been quite typical...

  Ernest and I begin at six with Bible study
  and Quiet Time in bed. I don't mean just sitting quietly.
  Quiet Time is our spiritual practice.
  First, we write down our emotions from the previous day.

Any troubling thoughts. For example, *that* morning,
I felt – misunderstood on a chat show.
Now this next part is quite nifty.
You take the feeling. Whatever it is.
And you hold it to the light like a five-pound note
and you ask that feeling four questions:

Is this absolutely honest?
Is this absolutely selfless?
Is this absolutely loving?
Is this absolutely pure?

And if the feeling fails on any one of those counts,
it is a false feeling
and I may surrender it to God.

'I felt misunderstood on a chat show.'

Is that absolutely honest? Yes.
Absolutely selfless? No.

Because my work is not about me. Ah-ha.
It's about giving my life to the Lord.
So that feeling fails on the second count – false feeling.
Surrender to God. Poof.

And the stillness returns. See?

That was a quick one, some mornings take longer.

Then I go down in my housecoat to make the tea, half an hour's weeding before breakfast, toast and marmalade, one slice, can never manage two. And *that* particular morning, I remember, my assistant was late. So. No one was in the office yet, and I was quite alone when this thing arrived in my life…

4

A ROMAN CENTURION *enters*.

CENTURION. As they took him from the cross,
 I took him in my arms.
 Beardless, breathless,
 he was still warm.
 They prepared the tomb,
 I kept guard over him
 then his mother and Mary Magdalene
 went to fetch clean linen
 to shroud his nakedness
 and we were alone for the last time.
 I kissed his mouth,
 my tongue found his, bitter with death
 then I took off my uniform
 and laid together with him
 in his desolation,
 hugging him,
 trying to warm him back to life.
 It was the only way I knew
 to speak our love's proud name, to tell him
 of my long devotion.
 I laid my lips around the tip
 of that great cock –

MARY. Nooooooooooooooo!

 He does *what* to the dead body of Christ?

 I said, ERNEST, IT'S FINALLY HAPPENED!

 They went too far.

 And what happens when the pendulum swings too far?

 We push back.

5

The NVALA annual conference.
MARY *comes on stage to great applause.*

MARY. Welcome to the annual conference of the National Viewers' and Listeners' Association. What a turn-out: from Inverness to Bognor Regis. All of us, ordinary people, simply viewing and listening to what comes out of our televisions, radios, cinemas and newsstands; it takes tremendous courage to expose yourself to this material and I thank you for everything you send me. There's a lot of light in this room, a lot of light, and my gosh are we going to need it – (*Her tone changes.*) in these Last Days, as prophesied in the Book of Daniel, when every true Christian is conscripted to fight the allied forces of the devil. The godless media call this 'a culture war'. It's not. It's a spiritual war. Light against darkness. Good against – (*Holds up* Gay News.) evil. We should have seen this coming. Jesus is the last hope these young men have of freeing their souls. So, of course, the homosexual lobby want to corrupt him. Jesus is their biggest threat! You see? If they convert Christ, they've won.

A huge amateurish banner drops down behind her, depicting Mary Whitehouse's face alongside Adolf Hitler's.

PROTESTERS. Two, four, six, eight, end the heterosexual state!

MARY. Ladies and gentlemen, we've been infiltrated.

MARY *turns around to look at the banner.*
Beat.

I've seen better artwork in primary schools! (*Taking back control of her audience.*) Calm down, they're only proving us right. (*Stretching her arms out like Christ.*) 'All who desire to live godly in Jesus Christ *will* suffer persecution.'

MARY *rips the banner down.*
Huge applause.

6

MARY (*to the audience*). Predictably, the *Guardian* launched a fighting fund for *Gay News*, claiming it 'could not possibly compete with Mary Whitehouse and her backers'. What backers? I had to trust that God would provide. But it wasn't the thousands of pounds of donations that moved me most. No. It was the mothers who reached out, during that time, asking *me* for help.

A Christian wives' coffee morning in her home – invitation only.

CECILIA. It all started when I was cleaning my daughter's room and I accidentally found a draft of a letter that she'd written to to... to the Archbishop of –

MARY (*jumping in*). A bold move for a young girl –

CECILIA. Maria's not a bad person honestly, she babysits our neighbour's children for free, she plays the flute –

MARY. The flute isn't relevant right now, Cecilia.

CECILIA. Oh.

MARY. Would you like me to read it?

CECILIA (*reading the letter*). 'My name is Maria and I am a twenty-one-year-old student currently studying Biology at Oxford.'

MARY. Biology. (*Under her breath.*) Oh the irony.

CECILIA (*reading*). 'Recently, I have lived through an experience that has made me doubt the humanity and kindness of the Church.'

MARY. Notice the entitled tone.

CECILIA (*reading*). 'When I moved to Oxford, away from my family, and joined the Women's Liberation Movement, I met a fascinating classicist called Sarah and we were good friends for a couple of months and then we fell in love and she became my lover. But she was a very devout Christian and had a lot of problems with her family and last September, she took an overdose and she died and that was a terrible shock' –

MARY (*interrupting*). That's enough. Firstly, are you alright, Cecilia?

CECILIA. I just... I just... I just feel so alone.

MARY. Look around. What do you see? Poppy, Mildred, Elsie... sorry, Elsbeth. Your new friends.

CECILIA. Thank you.

MARY. No, thank *you* – all – for visiting me. No mean feat. To admit this... about your own children. To agree to speak of it, out loud, with others? That takes tremendous strength. So when you found this letter, Cecilia, what did you do?

CECILIA. I sat at the top of the stairs for ten minutes – an hour – I don't know – then I heard this this this roaring sound... and realised the hoover was still plugged in.

MARY. And how did you feel?

CECILIA. Sad.

MARY. Betrayed. Scared. Angry at all the secrets she'd been keeping.

CECILIA. But she says this is who she is.

MARY (*sighs*). What is this modern obsession with the 'self'? Everybody clamouring, 'Look at *me*. Understand *me*. Listen to *me*' –

CECILIA. But the overdose –

MARY. I'm speaking now. In the forties, ladies, did we *ever* start a sentence with 'This is who I am'? We'd be laughed out of the room for being tremendously silly, for putting *ourselves* above the good of the community.

CECILIA. I just want her to like me again.

MARY. Cecilia!

CECILIA. Sorry.

MARY. Before she went to Oxford, Maria was completely normal, correct?

CECILIA. Well, I...

MARY *clearly wants her to say yes, so she says yes.*

Yes.

MARY. And it's not *just* about clothes, but what does Maria wear now?

CECILIA. Thick jumpers. Corduroy trousers.

MARY. And which political group did she join?

CECILIA. The Women's, erm, Liberation –

MARY. Have you heard of 'The Web'?

CECILIA *blinks.*

Anyone? The Web?

Little beat.

Thank goodness you're here.

MARY *displays 'The Web' diagram (a complex spider-diagram visually demonstrating how multiple departments and organisations – dealing in matters of sexual and mental health, family planning, women's rights and gay rights – are all linked in terms of funding and influence).*

Understand, we are not dealing with a solitary poor homosexual – for whom I have nothing but sympathy – but rather a network of highly connected minorities burrowing under the fabric of our society. Sex education used to be simple, 'Chastity before marriage and fidelity within it' until groups such as the British Humanist Society and the prophylactic-pushers at the Brook Advisory Centre began pressurising the Ministry of Education to include their propaganda in textbooks, and these same people write for teenage magazines, they're youth workers, agony aunts, switchboard operators, feminist group leaders. All webbed together. For example – Cecilia, concentrate! – the Campaign for Homosexual Equality is inextricably linked to the National Association of Mental Health, or 'Mind', because sixty-four per cent of 'gays' suffer from psychiatric issues (unsurprisingly, as homosexuality *is* a mental and spiritual illness). Yet are they *helped*? Cured of their delusion? No. They're enabled, encouraged. *Because* Mind is funded by the Department of Health and Social Security which leads straight to the Family Planning Association which shares an address with the Birth Control Trust which profits from the contraceptive lobby which, in turn, fills the coffers of the London Rubber Industries. Condoms. I'm getting too technical. But they're all connected, as you can see, with the abortion lobby in the middle there. And what is the objective, shared by all of these affiliates? Mildred?

Little beat. She rephrases the question.

Elsbeth. What do they all want?

Little beat.

Come on, ladies, it's literally staring you in the face. Look. What is their common purpose, Cecilia?

CECILIA *looks baffled.*

The destruction of the family.

CECILIA. Gosh.

MARY. Once you see it, you can't unsee it.

CECILIA. So what do I do?

MARY. Finally, the right question! Well done, Cecilia, we got there in the end. The first step is naming it for what it is…

7

MARY (*to the audience*). People think I've never known a homosexual but it's simply not true. I loved my friend Henry dearly. Henry was a good Christian, he wanted a family, children…

1932. A meeting room of the Oxford Group (*later known as the Moral Re-Armament Movement.*) *HENRY* (*a friend of Young Mary*) *has been stacking chairs.*

HENRY. I've laid out the biscuits, the coffee is brewed and today is my one-year anniversary free from… my former self.

MARY (*observing her own memory*). Remember, you are doing the right thing.

HENRY. I keep on having this dream where I go to the mirror and think something is wrong with my face and then I realise I have no pupils in my eyes. No dots. Not even pinpricks, just iris. Just these blank green discs staring back at me and I don't know where I've gone, I don't know how to find… myself in my eyes. I don't know where I am, Mary, I don't know where I am.

MARY. Hold fast.

8

MARY *is suddenly on her own in the garden, disorientated.*

'Bridge over Troubled Water' starts playing.

MARY. Ernest, did you switch the radio on?

Strange. Switch it off.

She picks up her binoculars.

Switch it off.

The music stops.

(*Looking through binoculars.*)
A pale young man in a brown, tailored suit.
A man in makeup and a spangly leotard thingy.
More hard-faced women.
A floppy-haired boy in a stripy shirt...
can't be more than nineteen.

9

Birmingham university. 1977.

MARY. Hello, hello, nice to see you all, thanks to the Birmingham Student Union for inviting me, always a pleasure to speak to the bright young minds of the future. I didn't go to university myself. At my school I was held up for years as an example of how *not* to sit an examination! But I did go to teachers' training college. And, though my opponents make me out to be against creativity, I in fact taught art! Oh yes. Children turned up to my class with little bags of bark, petals, leaves, cloth, paper and glitter. Remember when you were children? Not long ago, was it? Well, these days, children are exploited, not in coal mines or cotton mills, but in the factory of ideas.

JACOB (*from the auditorium*). Mrs Whitehouse.

MARY (*trying to ignore the interruption*). A nation's youth is its greatest asset –

JACOB (*from the auditorium*). Mrs –

MARY. – and if we do not ensure their inalienable right to childhood –

JACOB stands up.

JACOB. Mrs Whitehouse!!!

MARY. Yes, young man? Ooh I love a question. (*Beckoning to him*.) Come on up.

JACOB *was not expecting this.*
JACOB *comes forward and steps up onto the stage beside her.*
MARY *hands him the microphone.*

JACOB. My name... I'm a student, I'm second year, studying music. For you to claim, Mrs Whitehouse, that the *Gay News* –

MARY (*sighing*). This again –

JACOB. – blasphemy trial has nothing to do with homophobia is, in my mind, the most egregious misrepresentation of the facts. Gay people are clearly an ana... an anathema to you...

Overcome with emotion, he departs from his prepared speech.

You see me, this is what I am. I am a homosexual. I shake like this and I weep because I'm so frightened. I go in fear and trembling for my life because of you. I know that I'm going to be killed. And it's all your fault, your fault.

JACOB *drops the microphone.*

It's all your fault.

JACOB *runs offstage.*

MARY *takes back control of her audience.*

MARY (*laughing*). Goodness! No, no. I'm quite alright. Honestly, I'm used to it. It's alright. I'm alright.

10

A music practice room in the university.

JACOB *is sitting at the piano, crying. He's still holding the piece of paper with his speech on it.*

MARY *knocks lightly and enters.*

MARY. Room for a little one?

She closes the door behind her.

Your music teacher said I might find you in a practice room.

Beat.

Some big words out there. Big feelings.

JACOB. I don't have anything to say to you.

MARY. No? Because it seemed like you were just getting started.

She creeps closer.

Is that your prepared speech?

JACOB. I didn't say it.

MARY. I gathered.

JACOB throws the crumpled-up piece of paper in her general direction.

MARY looks at him.

JACOB. Sorry.

MARY (*uncrumpling his speech*). Egregious.

She gently folds the speech and puts it in her pocket.

My name's Mary, what's yours?

JACOB. Why do you care?

MARY gives him a look.

Jacob.

MARY. And what are you practising, Jacob?

She leans over his shoulder.

(*Not familiar with it*.) Simon and Garfunkel.

JACOB. You don't know 'Bridge over Troubled Water'?

MARY. No but the title reminds me of a psalm.

JACOB. Thanks, I don't need –

MARY. One-four-seven. He heals the brokenhearted and binds up their wounds.

JACOB. No, he doesn't. He *causes* wounds if anything. My friend Paul went for a walk and was hospitalised for a week. They left a bootprint on his face.

Pause. Every time JACOB *gets angry,* MARY *lets it hang in the air and* JACOB *then feels embarrassed/over-emotional.*

MARY. And you think I want that to happen to you, Jacob? Because that is what you said, out there, in front of all those people.

JACOB. You want me to not exist.

MARY. Jacob, I not only want you alive, I want you happy and safe. Would it surprise you to know that I too have suffered from sinful desires?

JACOB. You're a lesbian?

MARY. No. I was referring to a different type of temptation, equally condemned in the Bible. Nevertheless, I really did feel – for a brief second – that that feeling, that false joy, was 'who I was'.

JACOB. You think something is wrong with me.

MARY. Yes.

JACOB *scoffs, surprised by her bluntness*.

And so do you.

JACOB *shakes his head*.

Deep down.

She comes closer.

Look how much pain you're in. Riddled with shame, and fear.

JACOB. Because of you.

MARY. Really? A grandmother who collects pebbles?

She comes closer.

Hanky?

She passes him a hanky.

Are you close to your mother?

Beat.

Oh I'm sorry, touched a nerve. Let's change the subject. Sing me a little of your song.

JACOB. What?

MARY (*affectionately, winking*). Don't say 'what' say 'pardon'. Please.

JACOB. I'm not… I'm not singing for you.

MARY. You want to teach me, don't you? My horizons can be broadened too, you know. Please.

JACOB *starts playing*.

Lovely.

JACOB *sings the first verse and chorus of 'Bridge over Troubled Water'*.

He stops.

Et cetera.

MARY. Hmmm.

JACOB. You hate it.

MARY. Not at all. I see a lot of myself in you. You're lost but you're searching –

JACOB. It's just part of my contemporary music module.

MARY. No, no. Jacob. That was a prayer.

JACOB. I'm sorry I said those things about you.

MARY. I know.

JACOB. I'm sorry, I'm so sorry, I'm just so frightened…

MARY *embraces him*.

MARY. Promise me. Tonight. You'll go home.

JACOB. Home?

MARY. Your poor mother, worried sick. It's very simple. Go home, get down on your knees and ask for God's forgiveness…

JACOB *runs out, crying*.

Jacob…

Enter RICHARD BIRCH, *youth counsellor.*

(*To the audience.*) It was at this point that a much older, bigger 'youth counsellor' pushed his way into the room.

RICHARD. What the hell did you say to him?

MARY. That's between him and me.

RICHARD. I've done a lot of work with that young man on self-acceptance.

MARY. Oh, I bet you have. Counsellor? Corruptor, more like.

RICHARD. What lies behind your smile is repulsive indeed.

MARY. Just go away. You're a virus. (*To the audience.*) These are the people we must fight: the ideologues, the indoctrinators and their fanatical *cult* that will not stop until everyone is homosexual, even Jesus Christ.

11

4th July 1977. Outside the Old Bailey.

NEWS REPORTER. Mrs Mary Whitehouse arrives at court, ten a.m., in a burgundy blouse, gold earrings, a baby-blue jacket and a bright-pink silk scarf.

MARY (*to the audience*). The gays were not expecting that.

PROTESTERS. Whitehouse! Out! Whitehouse! Out! Whitehouse! Out!

MARY (*to the audience*). Anyone would've thought *I* was the accused, on trial for my sins against sodomy.

MARY *smiles wider, as if they are cheering her.*

But as they shouted, I just smiled.

And as they shouted louder, I smiled wider. After all, it was rather amusing them all shouting 'out, out, out' as I was quite literally going *in* to the Old Bailey.

Inside the Old Bailey.

COURT CLERK. Whitehouse versus Denis Lemon and Gay News Ltd. All rise. Court is now in session.

MARY (*to the audience*). The first day was incredibly distressing for all the Christians in the court.

GEOFF ROBERTSON. Before the indictment is put in this case, my Lord, I have an application to quash. There has been no trial for blasphemy for over half a century. Christianity is no longer part and parcel with the state. The law itself is obsolete.

MARY (*to the audience*). Imagine how we felt, listening to that. Obsolete. Obsolete. Says this leftie lawyer in his fancy wig, telling all of us little people that our religion is irrelevant and old-fashioned and the moral fabric of Britain has *already* decayed – it's not the wool of lambs any more, it's tie-dye and leather. Luckily, the judge was having none of it and our trial – God's will – was allowed to proceed.

JOHN SMYTH. Members of the jury, if you stroll into any branch of WHSmiths or local newsagent's in Britain, you will be able to buy for twenty-five pence, a newspaper called *Gay News*...

MARY (*to the audience*). When I first met our prosecuting barrister, John Smyth, at his beautiful home in Winchester, I couldn't believe my luck. What a religious man. In his spare time, he runs Christian holiday camps for public schoolboys. Some he even invites to his home for one-to-one guidance; takes them into his garden shed, leads them through a process of atonement, and according to his wife, the boys come out profoundly altered. He was eager to take my case pro bono.

JOHN SMYTH (*to the jury*). We see from its front page that it boasts 'the world's largest circulation newspaper for homosexuals'. In this issue from June of last year, it published a poem in the middle of the newspaper which is the subject of this prosecution for the offence of blasphemous libel. That is 'blasphemy in writing'. First, it portrays Jesus Christ as a promiscuous homosexual.

(*Reading.*) I knew he'd had it off with Herod's guards,
Pontius Pilate, John the Baptist,
the rest of the twelve, together and apart.
He loved *all* men,
body and soul,
even me.

Next, it takes the crucifixion and makes it the scene for an act, not of ordinary buggery – if you can call it that – but buggery with the dead.

During the next part, MARY *subtly covers her ears.*

(*Reading, with a disgust bordering on enjoyment.*)
I laid my lips around the tip
of that great cock
and the shaft still throbbed.
His dear broken body was all
open wounds and in each wound,

his side, his back, his mouth
I came and came and came
as if each coming was my last

Looks up from the text and stares at the audience.

(*Reading.*)
then the miracle possessed us,
I felt him enter into me, and fiercely spend
his spirit's final seed within my hole,
my soul, unto the ends of the earth,
he crucified me with him
into kingdom come.

Now, members of the jury, do you like this poem? Or are you part of the vast majority of decent people?

MARY (*to the audience*). I felt we weren't really in a court at all, but somewhere where the great spiritual truths of Christendom were being fought out. (*Kneeling.*) Meanwhile, all over the country, believers met and prayed.

12

MARY. Lord, we pray for each person involved in the gay movement in this land.

SOFT-SPOKEN BRISTOLIAN WOMAN. Lord, we know that these dear men have sunk so low because of the work of Satan and sin within the human heart.

CONFIDENT YOUNG WELSHMAN. We want your power to be made known to them, Father. Each and every one.

ELDERLY WOMAN FROM THE EAST END. Father, we want you to come into their lives.

YOUNG YORKSHIRE MAN WITH SLIGHT LISP. We do pray that, throughout this trial, your name will be upheld.

OLD IRISH MAN. And grant our God and Father, that 'ere they pass out into eternity that these dear men may find the Lord Jesus.

MARY. Otherwise, what a – what an embarrassing situation, Lord, later in eternity, to face the Son of God.

13

The Old Bailey.

MARY (*to the audience*). The next day, Geoffrey Robertson, the celebrity leftie lawyer, rocked up with a Bible in his hand.

GEOFFREY ROBERTSON (*to the jury*). Ladies and gentlemen, I have the privilege of representing *Gay News*. The newspaper has been charged with attacking Christianity. It has been charged with doing so in an outrageous way. A way that would make a sympathiser's blood boil, and perhaps even endanger the peace. I have to show you this poem is nothing of the sort. This is no lavatory limerick. This is a genuine expression of how one man, a soldier, an outcast, an unbeliever, found Christian love and salvation. Christ loved all men, body, soul and spirit, 'even me'. Those are the two most important words in the poem. If he loved all men, he loved outcasts, sinners – (*Dramatic pause.*) even homosexuals.

MARY (*to the audience*). The audacity. To reframe that filth as a parable? This smooth-talker was trying to beat us with our own Bible.

GEOFFREY ROBERTSON (*to the jury*). Then you see in the penultimate stanza, the words 'with the hope of resurrection', and that is really what the poem is getting at. Now, is that a violent suggestion? It came from Christ's own teaching, didn't it? When he said he came to save sinners? The people who were outcast. Yes, members of the jury, even homosexuals have the opportunity, have the hope, of salvation.

Reflective pause.

I ask you to bring in a verdict of not guilty.

MARY (*to the audience*). I thought, how can the jury resist that? How can they resist it? And, for the very first time, I came face to face with the possibility that the case might be lost…

14

MARY. All Saturday, I trembled in my lawn chair, conscious I was sitting at a crisis point in history. Permit this poem and the floodgates would open.

I endured thirty seconds of *The Kenny Everett Show* before writing a letter of complaint.

I could feel the darkness gathering. Every perversion imaginable. Like a horde on the horizon looming larger and larger. And, that night, I was visited by a terrible dream.

My first classroom in Wolverhampton.
Crayon drawings adorned the walls.
But when I looked closer,
they weren't mummies and daddies.
Two women and a toddler. Two men and a baby.
And it wasn't my name on the blackboard.

DENIS LEMON. Gather round my ankles, children.

MARY. Dressed in fishnets, with giant fake plastic breasts, cradling a suckling piglet. Denis Lemon, the editor of *Gay News*.

DENIS LEMON. In the handkerchief code, yellow means urine.

MARY. Now I've never met this man and he was too much of a coward to take the stand but, in my dream, he was bold as brass.

DENIS LEMON. Dildo lollipops for everyone!

MARY. Teaching *my* class.

DENIS LEMON. This story is called 'Rosebud'. Once upon a time, Timmy's anus –

MARY. Then he saw me.

DENIS LEMON. You! It's you!

MARY. And all the children turned their little faces, each tattooed with a spider's web.

15

COURT CLERK. Members of the jury, do you find *Gay News* guilty or not guilty of blasphemous libel?

FOREMAN. Guilty.

MARY (*to the audience*). The blessed words of the judge will be forever imprinted on my soul…

JUDGE. This poem is quite appalling. I hope that, by this verdict, the pendulum of public opinion may swing back to a healthy climate.

16

11th July 1977. Victory speech on the steps of the Old Bailey.

MARY. I am rejoicing today. I am rejoicing today because Our Lord is no longer being vilified. I am rejoicing today because religious feelings are the essence of people.

Halfway through her speech, the phone starts ringing. MARY *is distracted/glitching between time periods/situations.*

And I am rejoicing today because this landmark ruling is the application on earth of the law of God.

RICHARD (*on the phone*). My name is Richard Birch. I am a youth counsellor at Birmingham University. We met yesterday. You called me a virus.

MARY. How I can help?

RICHARD. You can't and you don't.

MARY. I'm sorry?

RICHARD. You should be because he went home from your talk and took a Stanley knife to his wrists.

MARY. Who are you talking about?

Pause.

Not Jacob?

Why? What did you say to him?

RICHARD. What did *I* say?

MARY. He was strong when I left, he was clear, he was going home to pray. What did you do?

RICHARD. You really don't understand at all, do you?

MARY. Which hospital? I'll send him a card.

RICHARD. You stay the hell away from him.

MARY. No, *you* stay away. 'Youth counsellor.' You have blood on your hands.

RICHARD. Funny because that's exactly what I'm calling to say to you.

MARY. Well, one of us is wrong.

RICHARD. Yes.

MARY. It's not me.

RICHARD. But what if it is? What if it is? Can you imagine what it means if you're wrong, Mary Whitehouse, the damage you have caused?

MARY. Can you imagine if *you're* wrong?

RICHARD. Yes! I've been imagining it my whole life, like every gay person I know. You forget, we know you – you're not original – we have lived with you, and everyone like you, inside our heads, since forever, because you *are* shame, you're shame in human form.

MARY. I don't need this fanatical / preaching –

RICHARD. He nearly died.

MARY. Because of *your* ideology.

RICHARD. What if you're wrong? What if you're wrong? What if you're wrong? (*Continues repeating on an audio loop.*) What if you're wrong?

MARY *smiles and smiles and smiles*.

17

1932. Mary's childhood home. BEATRICE *(Mary's mother) has been drinking a cocktail on the sofa, reading* Time and Tide. *Duke Ellington is playing on the gramophone.* YOUNG MARY *(twenty-two) has just come in the door.*

YOUNG MARY. What is that noise?

BEATRICE. Duke Ellington. Do you like it?

> YOUNG MARY *looks at her for a moment.*
>
> *She picks up* BEATRICE*'s drink and sniffs it.*

It's a peach cobbler.

YOUNG MARY. At two p.m.?

BEATRICE. Would you like one?

YOUNG MARY. You've very kind, Mother, but our car is waiting. I'm just after a few sentimental items. My tennis trophies and so on.

BEATRICE. Don't be silly, sit down, I haven't seen you in months. Wait, what car?

> BEATRICE *looks out of the window.*

Who's he?

YOUNG MARY. Would you mind awfully if we turned off that racket? I can barely hear myself think.

BEATRICE. Are you teaching at a new school?

YOUNG MARY. In a manner of speaking. So this is what you've chosen, is it? This lifestyle.

BEATRICE. Look. If this is about your father and me, then we met for a cup of tea last week and both agreed, we're thriving.

YOUNG MARY. There's plates in the sink and you're not even dressed.

BEATRICE. Your father's painting again. I met his new lady friend.

YOUNG MARY. You did what?

BEATRICE. Sod it. I'm bored of being angry.

YOUNG MARY. Right well you've clearly lost your mind. But the darkest hour comes just before the dawn and I am here to bring you to the light.

BEATRICE. You're not talking like yourself.

YOUNG MARY. I don't know what you mean, Mother.

BEATRICE. Are you alright?

YOUNG MARY. Are you? Jazz. Cocktails.

BEATRICE. I'm happier now than I've ever been.

YOUNG MARY. Happier than your wedding day? Happier than the births of your children? I see.

BEATRICE. No, you don't 'see' anything because you're twenty-two.

A car horn beeps outside.

He's from that group, isn't he?

YOUNG MARY. Where's my birth certificate?

BEATRICE. Why?

YOUNG MARY. I may need it in the future.

BEATRICE. Listen. I'm not sure about these people you've been hanging about with. You do know they're not Church of England? I looked them up in the library and they're –

YOUNG MARY. They warned me you would do this. From the instant I walked in, you've been trying to plant doubt. But I know what I must do.

BEATRICE. Where are you going?

YOUNG MARY. I have given up my job to pursue a higher calling.

BEATRICE. What?

YOUNG MARY. Ernest and I will travel the country for five years, maybe more, sharing and guiding, and then we will get married and have children like the Lord wants.

BEATRICE *looks out of the window.*

BEATRICE. He looks about eighteen. And why's he dressed like a Victorian businessman?

YOUNG MARY. Oh no. That's not Ernest, that's Henry.

BEATRICE. Who's Henry?

YOUNG MARY. He used to be a homosexual. Ernest is waiting for us at the communal house.

BEATRICE. The communal house?

YOUNG MARY. I've saved fourteen souls already, Mother. Henry was my first.

YOUNG MARY *looks proudly out of the window.*

Now look at him.

BEATRICE. You can't give up work. Everyone at that school says you're the best teacher they've ever had.

YOUNG MARY. My spiritual work *is* work.

BEATRICE. It won't be enough.

YOUNG MARY. I *am* teaching – the process of soul surgery.

BEATRICE. I'm sorry, what? Soul surgery?

YOUNG MARY. Let no day pass without its season of silent waiting before God. We are a ministry of ordinary people who all muck in with the washing and cooking, changing the world through personal evangelism and, like a *proper* family, never put selfish feelings first. Will you atone?

BEATRICE. I love you.

Beat.

I should've said that more often.

YOUNG MARY. Not my question.

BEATRICE. Please stop smiling like that. That's not your smile.

YOUNG MARY. Will you atone? One last chance.

BEATRICE. For who I was? Yes. Not for who I am now.

YOUNG MARY. Then I will never see you again. But please don't worry.

YOUNG MARY *goes to leave*.

BEATRICE. Is this about Mr Morris?

YOUNG MARY *stops*.

That's his name, yes? Robert Morris? The man, the married man, you're actually in love with? Robert. Heartbreak is agony. But a cult and a new husband is a pretty drastic cure.

YOUNG MARY. This has nothing to do with him.

BEATRICE. It's got nothing to do with you losing two stone in a month, writing a hundred letters, crying all of the salt out of your body...

YOUNG MARY. Exactly. It was killing me.

BEATRICE. Because you ended it, didn't you? But what if you hadn't? He loves you, doesn't he? Who cares what society thinks?

YOUNG MARY. His children. And his wife.

BEATRICE. Love is / complicated.

YOUNG MARY. No, no, no, no, no, no, no. All I ever wanted, my whole childhood, was a happy home.

BEATRICE. That's not true. You *wanted* to be a tennis champion. Then you *wanted* to go to university and be a geologist. Always coming home with buckets of pebbles –

YOUNG MARY. What's this got to do / with anything?

BEATRICE. Always racing hell for leather on your bike, yanking the ribbon from your hair. Dad said you'd got his wayward spirit –

YOUNG MARY. I have *not* got his spirit!

BEATRICE. No, Mary, you've got mine, and you'll go mad. I got married before I knew who I was. A wife behaves so, a husband does thus.

YOUNG MARY. I don't want to hear this.

BEATRICE. I was a doll, a machine designed for changing nappies and making up bottles. I was not nice to be near, I was in no way a mother, I was in no way a person. Don't ruin your life, running away from yourself.

YOUNG MARY. You're right about one thing.

Little beat.

You were in no way a mother.

BEATRICE. Things are changing, Mary! We don't have to ignore our hearts any more!

YOUNG MARY. My heart?

Laughs.

Oh, you don't understand *at all*. You think Robert is the extent of my heart? Or Ernest for that matter? You think I'm doing this for a man?

BEATRICE. Well, aren't you?

YOUNG MARY. Henry, start the car! (*To* BEATRICE.) God has a plan for everyone's life and, if you listen, he will show you what it is.

BEATRICE. At least give me your new address.

YOUNG MARY. What for? You don't even know me.

18

'This Is My Life' by Shirley Bassey plays.

YOUNG MARY *transforms into the* MARY WHITEHOUSE *we know, dressed in a signature outfit, ready to take on the world.*

Interval.

19

As the house lights go down – light entertainment music.

TV CONTINUITY ANNOUNCER.
Whenever the world forgets its manners,
whenever innocence is under threat,
she is there,
a bastion of common sense,
campaigning in the corridors of power,
jetting around the globe,
bringing words of comfort
to ordinary people just like her.
Interrupting her busy schedule
to be with us this evening,
all the way from the UK,
ladies and gentlemen,
Mrs Mary Whitehouse!

The huge welcoming applause of a studio audience as the curtains open…

20

1986. Ten Downing Street.

MARGARET. Mrs Whitehouse. I've got some leftovers here from my lunch with the Governor of the Bank of England, if you'd like some cold ham?

MARY. Oh, you're just like me, Prime Minister. A mother hen, always trying to feed people.

MARGARET. Please, sit.

MARY. I was just admiring the photograph of your twins when they were little. Such plump, healthy faces. Who'd have thought it? Number Ten Downing Street, furnished with a woman's touch. That iconic front door. My cameraman *was* waiting to photograph us together… so I was quite surprised when your Chief of Staff directed me to the back entrance?

MARGARET. How can I help you, Mrs Whitehouse?

MARY. Mary, please. First things first –

MARY *takes out a cake tin containing a Victoria sponge.*

MARGARET. Gosh, an entire cake.

MARY. Shall I be Mother?

MARGARET THATCHER *places the cake tin on the side, unopened.*

Everyone always asks me, Mary, how do you get your sponge so light? Well, Margaret, the trick is warm butter. Leave a dish out in the sunshine for an hour. Or, on cold days, pop it on the radiator.

MARGARET. You shouldn't have.

MARY. But congratulations are in order! Belated, admittedly.

MARGARET. Yes, I'm sorry this meeting has taken so long to organise.

MARY. My point is, we banned the video nasties! Well done us. But, Margaret, that was two years ago now and the Home Secretary has yet to promise any new legislation on obscenity. We mustn't rest on our laurels. So, I have taken the liberty of bringing something to your attention.

MARGARET. Not another petition.

MARY *laughs, thinking* MARGARET *was joking.*

MARY (*handing over a large Tupperware box full of sex toys*). Now I'm not sure you know these things exist.

MARGARET *looks inside the box, pauses, closes it and hands it back.*

What if a child came across one of these in a bedside drawer? They'd be scarred for life. And many of them are brightly coloured, like children's toys. (*Taking one out.*) And this pink one comes with batteries. It vibrates, Prime Minister. Imagine inserting a battery-powered device into your private area.

MARGARET. I'd rather not.

MARY (*removing a large one from the box*). And look at the size of this! Not remotely anatomically correct, in my experience.

Beat.

Several of these could cause significant physical damage. As you can see.

MARGARET. Why am I staring at...

MARY (*returning it to the box*). I understand your reticence, Prime Minister. We've both been slammed, over and over, by the gavel of public opinion. And what a hilarious scene this would make on *Spitting Image* – our two grotesque puppets, brandishing... But you know something, Margaret? Whenever they call me a joke, or a prude, or a fascist, what I hear is, 'Mary, keep going.' Because sex is a joining of souls: it's intimacy, not industry. And British shops are selling these, in increasing numbers –

MARGARET. And why is that a government concern?

MARY. Excuse me?

MARGARET. They're all small businesses, quite skilful entrepreneurs some of them.

MARY. Surely you don't want *these* anywhere near our economy?

MARGARET. I'm not interested in what people do behind closed doors.

MARY. Of course you are. We're cut from the same cloth you and I, wives and mothers who stand for home and family which – by its very nature – lies behind a closed door. Where children live.

MARGARET. But this isn't a child protection issue.

MARY. Morality is *always* a child protection issue. Schoolchildren are putting condoms on bananas as we speak. They're teaching atheism in RE. How long before these barbaric instruments become part of the syllabus? Do you know what a buttplug is?

MARGARET. Mrs Whitehouse.

MARY. By letting these things be sold, we are encouraging DIY pornography. Just as we normalised sodomy in sixty-seven.

MARGARET. Oh, I don't think it's normalised.

MARY. Tell that to your education system. All over the country, children are being taught they have an inalienable right to be gay!

MARGARET. You don't need to worry about the homosexual agenda in schools any more, that is all in hand.

MARY. Really?

MARGARET. There'll be legislation within the year.

MARY. I would love to be involved in that process.

MARGARET. No need.

MARY. But… but I was one who told you about the social contagion, The Web…

MARGARET. And your input was invaluable. I do believe, in another life, you could've been a politician.

MARGARET *looks at her watch.*

MARY. Perhaps I will have a bit of that cold ham?

MARGARET. I'm so sorry. In the wake of the Chernobyl disaster, I've got to start thinking about my new nuclear contingency plan.

Beat.

But thank you for the baking tip. I'll remember that. (*Tapping her head.*) Warm butter.

21

Dressing room, backstage at Granada Studios.
MARY *is sitting, adjusting her makeup in the mirror.*

ADAM, *a vicar, is hovering in the doorway.*

MARY. Come in, come in, I don't bite.

> ADAM *comes slightly closer.*
>
> I thought I spied a vicar in the studio audience. I didn't know whether you'd come especially for me or if you were just a big fan of *Some You Win*. I'd never seen the show, had you?
>
> *He stares at her.* MARY *assumes he's starstruck.*
>
> Amusing format. 'Embarrassing blunders.' Although I am kicking myself for going with that 'salt in the crumble' story, when I've just remembered, last summer, I fell into my own septic tank. Right up to my waist. That would've been much funnier. Oh well. What's your name?

ADAM (*quietly*). Adam.

MARY. Forgive my clownish visage, Adam, they cake it on for the lights. In two minutes, I'll look human again then I promised I'd meet Lulu in the green room. Do you have a book for me to sign?

ADAM. When my twelve-year-old said the Scout leader was touching him, I knew it wasn't true.

MARY. Oh.

ADAM. The man was my deacon. I knew his character. My wife reported him to the bishop and he left town overnight, confirming the claims. But at least I knew the matter had been dealt with. I later found out he'd been transferred to a church in India, with a vast youth programme. What are you doing?

> MARY *is taking notes.*

MARY. For my research.

ADAM. That's not why I'm telling you.

MARY. You wouldn't catch the evangelicals behaving that way. It's these Anglican liberals preaching tolerance – of *what* exactly –

ADAM. Please just listen.

MARY *closes her notebook.*

When my son became a teenager, I noticed his comportment. Weak shoulders. The molestation had feminised him. My wife said, 'That's just who he is,' but she hadn't read the studies. I took him fishing, told him straight, 'If you choose this sinful lifestyle, your abuser will have won.' He cried but I knew the truth would set him free. It didn't. There were multiple incidents: a boy in his class, a dirty magazine in his satchel, bullies on the bus. I wanted him to be happy. Eventually, I said, if you can't lead a Christian life under my roof, you'll have to think about leaving. I never thought he would. Fifteen years later, I received a letter to say he was working with you on a documentary: 'Dad, I hope I've done something to make you proud.'

MARY. David. You're David's father.

ADAM. I wrote back immediately: 'If you have truly changed, come home for Christmas.' We bought a three-bird roast but he never showed. The years went by. My wife started visiting her sister all the time. Turns out, she was meeting him in secret. She'd heard me preach about AIDS, so when David got sick, she didn't tell me.

MARY. David's sick?

ADAM. No, actually, he died.

Little beat.

I turned to my wife at the wake, I said, see? Sin destroys families. She said, no, *you* destroyed our family.

ADAM *suddenly feels like he's been punched.*

MARY. Nonsense. God's word is truth and truth is love, therefore you were a loving father.

ADAM. It doesn't feel that way.

MARY. Feelings aren't facts. Return to your principles, that's what I do.

ADAM. I've spoken more to his gravestone than we spoke his entire adult life. I sit there for hours, talking rubbish to him. Always reuse tinfoil, son. Every sandwich needs a pickled onion. A Vauxhall Viva is the most reliable car. Keep your receipts.

MARY. But what use is that, vicar?

ADAM. I don't know.

MARY. Shouldn't you be praying for his soul?

ADAM. I don't know.

He bursts into tears.

I don't know, I don't know, I don't know, I don't know, I don't know.

He clutches on to her, bent over, crying.
It's messy.
He's getting tears on her clothes.

MARY (*gently*). So sorry but... my dress...

ADAM. Oh goodness, I... I... Sorry... I... I do apologise...

Mortified, ADAM *leaves as quickly as he can.*
MARY *is left alone.*

MARY (*clasping her hands together in prayer*). Dear Heavenly Father, I know mankind must be punished and that AIDS is my vindication, proof that sin ends in tragedy. But please take mercy on David's soul, for he was a lovely boy.

22

1987. Mary's garden. JILL TWEEDIE, *a journalist, is having tea with* MARY.

JILL. You may have read my *Guardian* column, 'Letters from a Faint-hearted Feminist,' with topics ranging from domestic violence to non-monogamy to the mud-caked women of Greenham Common. And now I find myself in front of you.

MARY. Hello, Mrs Tweedie.

JILL. Ms.

MARY. Hmm?

JILL. Ms.

MARY. Miss?

JILL. Ms Tweedie.

MARY. Muzz?

JILL. Call me Jill.

Beat.

(*Lighting a cigarette.*) As a feminist, I find you deeply confusing. My primal instinct is to admire your tenacious rowing against the tide.

MARY. Thank you.

JILL. And we overlap on certain issues –

MARY. Yes, so I wasn't surprised when you called. I gave a talk on 'sexploitation' at Cambridge last month and a group of 'women's libbers' raised their fists and shouted, 'Right on, Mary.'

JILL. Extraordinary.

MARY. Yes.

JILL. Like turkeys voting for Christmas.

MARY. I beg your pardon?

JILL. Because you're anti-feminist. Anti-abortion, anti-divorce, anti-contraception, anti-equal pay –

MARY. I'm not anti-anything, Mrs Tweedie. I'm *pro*-family. *Pro*-joy.

JILL *clicks play on her Dictaphone.*

JILL. The joy of sex?

MARY. Oh yes! Yes! Oh, you mustn't think people who speak out on these issues aren't happy in their sex lives. I am and always have been.

JILL. Really?

MARY. Although joy is not the same as pleasure. Joyful sex occurs within the context of an eternal spiritual bond. *That* is satisfaction. No need to light a cigarette afterwards.

JILL. So unmarried women can't experience sexual joy?

MARY. Sin cannot be joyous. Oxymoron, I'm afraid. (*Pushing the biscuits towards her.*) Garibaldi?

JILL. Do you get a kick out of telling other people how to behave?

MARY. A kick?

JILL. You've just come back from an international speaking tour. America, Australia –

MARY. It's campaigning, not cavorting. I wish I could simply stay home and tend the garden but –

JILL. *The Dame Edna Everage Show* –

MARY. Children are at risk –

JILL. *Celebrity Squares* –

MARY. I'm just an ordinary woman –

JILL. With an extraordinary web of influence: lawyers, lords, MPs –

MARY. I do not have a web –

JILL. – church leaders, senior police officers –

MARY. *Your* left-wing cult is recruiting our youth.

JILL. Aren't you from an actual cult?

MARY. I… The Moral Re-Armament Movement is a normal Christian fellowship.

JILL. Define normal.

MARY. Do you agree with child pornography?

JILL. No.

MARY. Well, I banned it. Write this down.

JILL doesn't take notes.

In seventy-eight, I pushed through that child protection law.

JILL. I don't agree with video nasties either, or horror on television before nine p.m.

MARY. There you go, we agree. 'Is Mary Whitehouse Right?' Not to pen your headline for you…

JILL. Oswald Mosley fought for old-age pensions and raising the school leaving age but I don't go around saying, 'Was Mosley right?'

MARY (*smiling*). Comparing me to a fascist –

JILL. My point is, you can't cherry-pick the views of Mary Whitehouse, can you? Because you stand for a wholesale ideology. A shame-based, religious fundamentalist, patriarchal belief-system of moral purity and biological determinism.

MARY (*smiling*). Goodness. I feel like I'm on trial.

JILL. I'm just naming it for what it is.

MARY. Please don't ash in my saucer.

JILL. Oh, I'm sorry.

MARY. I'll fetch you a ramekin.

Exit MARY.

JILL *takes the opportunity to look around the garden.*

Enter MARY, *with a ramekin.*

JILL. What about me then, on my third – finally happy – marriage, am I allowed joy in sex? Or is it relegated to mere animal pleasure?

MARY. I believe in the sanctity of first and only marriages.

JILL. And what is your position on orgasm equality?

MARY. On what?

JILL. The orgasm gap between men and women.

MARY. Look. Married couples have been having sex for centuries quite happily long before this overwhelming need to talk about it.

JILL. Do you even think women should vote?

Pause.

Oh my God, you're pausing!

MARY. It's a complex question.

JILL. Is it?

MARY. As we're *now* in a Britain of broken families and porn-addled men, women must vote, and juries should be fifty per cent female, especially for obscenity cases. But did the suffragettes begin our decline? Well. The Christian position was always that households should not be divided against each other. Man and wife share one vote, one voice. So, if you think about it, women's suffrage broke that bond, opening the door to all these other so-called permissive reforms.

Beat.

JILL. Wow.

Beat.

Well, now I'm thinking *are* you 'the most dangerous woman in Britain', or are you simply the last stand of a very old guard?

MARY. Oh, I wouldn't underestimate the old guard, Mrs Tweedie. Our last stand has lasted for a pretty long time.

JILL. In your twenties, you gave up your job as an art teacher to become a full-time housewife and mother to three boys.

MARY. Five boys.

JILL. Five?

MARY. Two are with Jesus.

JILL. Are you comfortable speaking on that?

MARY. Absolutely. I fell pregnant with twins and the doctor informed us that they would not survive.

JILL. And… were you encouraged to…?

MARY. Have an abortion. That's right.

JILL. To which you said –

MARY. Abortion is a sin.

JILL. I'm sorry, that must have been –

MARY. No, no, it was a blessing, I held both in my arms, named them and buried them; and I would encourage any woman to do precisely the same.

JILL. Despite the trauma you went through?

MARY. What trauma?

JILL. You're a tough nut to crack.

MARY. There's nothing to crack.

JILL. Can I say something mad?

Little beat.

Do you know the Bob Dylan lyric, 'We always did feel the same, we just saw it from a different point of view'?

Obviously, MARY *does not.*

You see, I have a theory. That, in another life, I could've become you and you could've become me.

JILL *passes* MARY *her cigarette. The actors swap roles.*

Hear me out. I had my first three children before I was twenty-five with a man I did not love. He was a tyrant, I was a ghost. I left. But what if I hadn't? If I rewind the tape back to twenty-five-year-old Jill, standing in the doorway with her bags packed. What if she'd turned around and gone back in that house? How would she have squared the paradox between the power inside her and the limitations of her life? She couldn't have carried on feeling like that and stayed sane. Oh no. To stay would've required a drastic new philosophy. That lack of self *was* her personality. Suppression *was* strength. And feminists? Oh, she'd have hated them. Mocking her sacrifice. Putting themselves first. But then maybe, when the children were grown and her husband's grip weakened with age, *that* Jill would've found a way to become what she always was – a speaker, a broadcaster, gushing with opinions; squashed down for years now springing up like a Jack-in-a-box, reaping all the rewards of feminism – respect, a platform – yet all the while, preaching the same message that stopped her walking out that door at twenty-five: 'Get back in your box. Put a lid on it. Your role *is* who you are.' Meanwhile, in a parallel life, Mary Whitehouse is reading Doris Lessing on a window ledge, smoking, three husbands in, writing a feminist column for the *Guardian*, having sex for pleasure and fighting the likes of me. All because, somewhere back in her twenties, she made a different choice.

The cigarette is passed back. The actors resume their original roles.

What do you think?

MARY *is smiling.*

MARY (*with a controlled rage that slowly builds throughout the speech*). Top marks for creativity. What a fascinating thought experiment. Must be marvellous to be so enlightened and liberated, musing on the roots of other women's – what did you say? – suppression. Yes. I tell people to 'put a lid on it'. For there is a depravity at the heart of man. And the more you feed it, the more it craves the forbidden. Once men were titillated by the flash of an ankle. Now topless photos barely arouse. Because you allowed it, with your 'freedom'. So now desires must darken to remain forbidden. First, it's page three, then it's rape –

JILL. Whoa, rape existed before page three –

MARY. Not on video, in technicolour, freely available to normal men – who may not rape but, by George, they'll watch it – image after image dilating the eyes like a drug, demanding more because the devil is always hungry, give him soft porn he wants hard porn, sadomasochism, bestiality, necrophilia, torture, paedophilia, murder, anything to feed that dark fire which, left unchecked, will build and build until the whole world is burning and women like you turn into women like me, begging them to 'put a lid on it'!

Little beat.

JILL. I... Would you mind terribly if I used your bathroom? And then I'll be on my way and leave you alone.

Exit JILL.
MARY *is left alone.*

23

1931. Wolverhampton. Meeting of the Oxford Group. YOUNG MARY *is twenty-one years old, sitting in the 'hot seat', and crying her eyes out.*

YOUNG MARY. I'm pathetic.
No, I'm not.
It's everything.
It's the meaning of life
and I found it
with Robert
briefly.

I can't explain.
No, I can.
Rhomb porphyry.
It's a rare pebble.
Don't smile at me.
I'm not a silly girl.
It's the holy grail of pebbles.
Smile again and I'm going.
This is *my* way of talking about *my* love.
Let me have that, at least. Please.
I found one once, on the Norfolk coast,
must have travelled all the way from Norway,
these diamond-shaped crystals
nestled in brown-black rock
and I picked it up,
I couldn't believe it.
Out of all the pebbles on that beach?
What are the chances?
He took me to a hotel.
It wasn't seedy.
Of course, I felt guilty.
No, I didn't.
I felt joy
and now you're asking me to take out my heart
full of rare joy
and just throw it back in the sea?
Well, I can't,
I won't do it.

ERNEST WHITEHOUSE. Then why are you here, Mary?

MARY *cries and cries.*

24

A few months later. Private room in the communal house.

YOUNG MARY (*referring to her clipboard*). My name is Mary Hutcheson and I am your designated soul surgeon. And your name is...

HENRY. Henry Bennett.

YOUNG MARY. Don't worry, Henry. There's no scalpels, I promise.

HENRY. Oh good.

YOUNG MARY. Um. (*Referring to her clipboard.*) Alright, so this follows the principles of personal evangelism, where one man – or woman – is the minister and one man is the congregation. It's about influencing individual souls to change lives. In five simple steps. Confidence, Confession, Conviction, Conversion, Conservation. The five Cs.

HENRY. Should I write this down?

YOUNG MARY. No need, sit back, relax. Number one: Confidence. (*Referring to her clipboard.*) 'The physician of souls must know his patients intimately, or he cannot diagnose their troubles accurately.' Sorry. I don't think I was meant to say that bit out loud. This is my first time.

HENRY. Me too.

YOUNG MARY. So... I guess... tell me everything about you.

HENRY. Just everything?

YOUNG MARY. Plus the kitchen sink.

HENRY. Um. I'm local. Obviously. I work at Isaac Millets in town.

YOUNG MARY. I know it.

HNERY. I'm treating it like a placeholder until a job comes up in Willerbys on Queen Square, that's my dream: (*Doing a posh tailor's voice.*) 'Never before has such fine tailoring been offered on such easy terms.' I also do one night a week at Priestley Piano shop.

YOUNG MARY. Do you play?

HENRY. Just silly stuff.
   (*Pretending to play the piano on his lap.*)
   Where did you get that hat?
   Where did you get that tile?
   Isn't it a nobby one and just the proper style?

Pause.

I'm nervous.

YOUNG MARY. And your parents?

HENRY. Are nearby. But. (*In one breath.*) So Dad didn't get into the army 'cause of his bad kidneys so now he's in the territorial and goes to all the weekly sessions at the Drill Hall on Newhampton Road but the Major keeps bringing him home 'cause he faints during training so he's angry all the time and apparently it's all my fault so I'm not allowed to visit till I've stopped being like this.

Breathes.

Whatever this is.

YOUNG MARY. And how old are you, Henry?

HENRY. Nineteen. And a half.

YOUNG MARY. And you don't live at home?

HENRY. No. Tudor Road, with three of the Millets girls.

YOUNG MARY. In Wednesfield?

HENRY. Yes.

YOUNG MARY (*pointing at herself*). Deans Road! How far do you walk for the trolleybus?

HENRY. Hundred yards.

YOUNG MARY. Same stop! I teach art at Lichfield –

HENRY. Really?

YOUNG MARY. I must've seen you before.

HENRY. We should go for a drink at The Lion.

YOUNG MARY. Yes.

Remembers where she is.

No. Henry. The next step is Confession.

Beat.

Why are you here?

HENRY. I have to say it?

YOUNG MARY. Afraid so.

HENRY. I have…

YOUNG MARY. It's alright.

HENRY. Unnatural thoughts about men.

YOUNG MARY. Great.

Beat.

I mean, good job.

HENRY. I'm done? I've confessed?

YOUNG MARY (*referring to her clipboard*). No, no, I must see fully into the darkened chamber.

HENRY. Sorry?

YOUNG MARY. Please recount every sinful thought or deed from your life.

They look at the clock. It's 8 p.m.

Don't worry, mine took two hours.

And some thoughts I didn't even know *were* sins…

Start anywhere.

HENRY. Erm… When I was seven, my mum said I needed cuddles too much. Is that something?

YOUNG MARY. Oh definitely.

Four hours later. Midnight.

HENRY. And then, yesterday, I nearly didn't come here at all 'cause the devil said, 'You're fine, carry on as you are.'

YOUNG MARY. Henry.

HENRY. Huh?

YOUNG MARY. You've done it.

HENRY. It's over?

YOUNG MARY. But Confession is not *Conviction* of sin. Stage three.

She takes his hand.

Repeat after me. 'Father, I have sinned against heaven.'

HENRY *can't say it.*

You have to say it.

Two hours pass. 2 a.m.

HENRY (*shouting*). I am unspiritual, the slave, bought and sold, of sin! I am no longer worthy to be called your son!

HENRY *throws up in the wastepaper basket.*

Another hour passes. 3 a.m.

YOUNG MARY. Are you ready for your new self to awaken, changing your heart, strengthening your will and illuminating your mind?

HENRY. Please just tell me what to do.

YOUNG MARY. Oh, I don't participate in this.

HENRY. Pardon?

YOUNG MARY. Conversion must occur in you alone.

HENRY. So what do I do?

YOUNG MARY. You're not already feeling it?

HENRY. Feeling what?

YOUNG MARY (*referring to her clipboard*). The burden of sin falling from your shoulders?

Pause. HENRY *is not feeling this, no.*

It must be already happening.

HENRY. Yes.

Beat.

Yes.

Two hours pass. 5 a.m.

YOUNG MARY. And finally, step five, Conservation.

(*Referring to her clipboard.*) To avoid backsliding, the new convert should receive the most sedulous attention in the days following. This means, daily practice.

HENRY (*broken*). *Daily* practice?

YOUNG MARY. We'll do it together the first week till it becomes second nature. (*Referring to her clipboard.*) As soon as you wake up, write down any troubling feelings from the previous day then, one by one, hold each to the light and ask that feeling four questions:

Is this absolutely honest?
Is this absolutely selfless?
Is this absolutely loving?
Is this absolutely pure?

And if the feeling fails on any one of those counts, it is a false feeling and you may surrender it to God.

HENRY. So that's all of them then.

YOUNG MARY. Sorry?

HENRY. Don't all feelings fail on one of those counts?

YOUNG MARY (*referring to her clipboard*). Erm.

HENRY. The room's blurry.

YOUNG MARY. You're backsliding already.

HENRY. Sorry.

YOUNG MARY. But the good news is, we're practically next-door neighbours! So I can visit you every single day.

HENRY. Thanks, Mary.

YOUNG MARY. No, thank *you*. I've saved my first soul. And the sun is coming out.

25

Mary's garden. 1987.

JILL. My cab will be here soon.

> MARY *is still transitioning between time periods/worlds.*

Thanks for letting me use your bathroom, I've got one of these awful glitzy book launches tonight and the time just whizzed past quite mysteriously.

MARY. It did rather.

JILL. Well, I've got about ten thousand words of material here – not sure it quite fits the brief… but what a beautiful garden to argue in.

MARY. Ten years ago, all I could see was an ocean of placards and angry young men.

JILL. Oh yeah?

MARY. How many are dead now, I wonder, or in hospital…

JILL. Are you joking?

MARY. Sorry?

JILL. *Gay News* was the only source of information for homosexuals, distributed nationally.

MARY. So?

JILL. So, after your privately funded trial, advertisers wouldn't touch them, WHSmiths stopped stocking them, and they went under in 1983 just before the epidemic hit. If it wasn't for you, there could've been information about AIDS on every newsstand in Britain. Instead, there was silence. How many boys do you think that killed?

MARY. Our interview is over, Mrs Tweedie.

JILL *(packing up)*. Sorry, Mrs Whitehouse, force of habit.

MARY. But that poem was blasphemous.

JILL. Of course it was.

MARY. Thank you.

JILL. And they had every right to be. Do you know how many times gay people have been fucked by Jesus?

MARY *gasps*.

MARY. You sound just like those protesters.

JILL. Pardon my French.

MARY. I'm alright. In the end, light always defeats darkness.

JILL. And which one are you?

MARY. Oh, oh. I have a drawer full of death threats. They compared me to Hitler. One man threatened to burn my house down. Whereas I have always been polite, patient and kind to homosexuals. I am a good person.

JILL. I know you are.

Beat.

And that's the problem. You're a good person, good citizen, good neighbour, good friend, good wife, good mother, good grandmother, good Christian. And then you look over at these troubled gay people, angry, desperate, ill, dressing strangely and shouting at you, and you think, 'How could *they* be on the right side of history?' When, look at you.

You're so composed and intelligent. And you have the Bible and history and legislation and biological textbooks and psychological studies and countless ordinary people all on *your* side.

MARY. Is this supposed to change my mind?

JILL. Exactly. How *do* you change the mind of a person like that? Banning you, threatening you, throwing custard pies at you – doesn't work. It just confirms your sense of persecution. And calling you Hitler... misses the point. Hitler was a monster. We want to believe that all oppression is carried out by bad people. But the scarier truth – is it's mostly done by good people, like you, who cannot accept, for the life of them, that they could ever be monstrous.

Beat.

MARY. I've never oppressed anybody.

JILL. My taxi's here.

MARY. *You've* been monstrous, permitting this world, but you can't admit it, because you're so worthy and progressive. Married *three* times, you said? All your life, just choosing the easy path? Chasing adventures and fun?

JILL. Fun?

MARY. Swigging cocktails in high heels, whilst children are at risk.

JILL *walks out, then walks straight back*.

JILL. My first husband was abusive and when I left, he kidnapped my two children and took them to Hungary. I spent twenty years of earnings all on legal fees. And when I finally saw them again, we spoke no common language. So, no, it wasn't fun.

MARY. I'm sorry.

JILL. A boy and girl. Adults now. I had another son but, erm, he died of cot death at five months old.

MARY. You should have said earlier.

JILL. Why?

MARY. Because, whatever our political differences, I can always relate to another mother's pain.

JILL. With respect, Mrs White… Mary. You can't even feel your *own* pain.

Exit JILL.

MARY *is left alone.*

She experiences a strange feeling that she doesn't know how to cope with.

MARY. Is this absolutely honest?
Is this absolutely selfless?
Is this absolutely loving?
Is this absolutely pure?

26

YOUNG MARY *is holding two dead babies, one in each arm.*

NURSE. Are you sure you don't wish to hold your babies for a little while longer, Mrs Whitehouse?

YOUNG MARY (*not crying*). They've gone now.
God needs them more than me.
You can take them now.
I'm done.
I mustn't be selfish.
This is a false feeling.
It's not about me.

NURSE. Take all the time you need.

YOUNG MARY. No, no.
I'm done.
And the house needs attending to.
You can take them now.
Thank you.

27

The radio switches itself on. The second verse of 'Bridge over Troubled Water' plays.

MARY. Switch it off.

The song keeps playing.

Switch it off! SWITCH IT OFF! SWITCH IT OFF! Help! Help!

JOSEPH. No shouting. And no one's switching anything off. This is the final, Mary, and everyone else wants to watch it.

We're in the television room of Abberton Manor. MARY *is ninety-one years old. A reality TV show is playing.*

MARY. Final? What final?

PRESENTER. You are the last two contestants in the house. Votes have been counted, and I can now reveal, with a total of four million, two hundred and thirty votes, Brian is this year's winner, I'm coming in.

CONTESTANT. Oh my oh my oh my god –

Whoops and cheers.

28

2001.

Abberton Manor nursing home.

A summer's night. 10 p.m.

MARY *has been wheeled out of the TV room by* JOSEPH, *a young gay nurse.*

MARY. I've been forcibly removed!

JOSEPH. I've just gently wheeled you out into the fresh air, Mary. The TV room is a democracy not a dictatorship.

MARY. You're the dictator, not me! This is discrimination. Am I not allowed to speak?

JOSEPH. Nobody's harassing you during *Gardener's World*, are they?

MARY. False equivalence. *Gardener's World* does not contain naked people in hot tubs. And why are you letting everyone stay up past ten p.m.?

JOSEPH. As a treat, Mary.

MARY. A treat for whom? This is all Edith's influence. *Her* favourite programme has hijacked my whole summer. Imagine watching idiots talk nonsense. Watching them sleep.

JOSEPH (*thinking 'that's basically my job'*). Imagine.

MARY. And you need to confiscate her tarot cards. She's been laying them out in the day room like a witch, brainwashing the weaker residents.

JOSEPH. I can't confiscate them, they're her spiritual practice.

MARY. Piffle, they're satanic. And she's addicted to Mills and Boon, she reads four, five a week then leaves them in the magazine rack, and now Yvonne and Shirley are reading them.

JOSEPH. I can't snatch books out of people's hands, Mary, they're adults.

MARY. Edith has single-handedly ruined this place.

JOSEPH. This is a communal home and we all need to adapt to accommodate each other.

MARY. Why should I adapt? I'm ninety-one.

JOSEPH. It's never too late.

MARY. But I'm *right*.

JOSEPH. So what are we going to do? You have to live together and you can't kill each other and you can't carry on like this.

Little beat.

What does the Bible say? 'Live and let live.'

MARY. That's not from the Bible.

JOSEPH. It is.

MARY. It isn't.

JOSEPH. To be fair, my Auntie Linda has it on a bumper sticker.

MARY. Oh well who needs papyrus scrolls and stone tablets when you have bumper stickers, fridge magnets and cereal packets? 'Look, the Holy Trinity: Snap, Crackle and Pop.'

JOSEPH laughs.

JOSEPH. You're funny.

Affectionate beat. MARY *puts her hand on his.*

Are you sure you're alright, Mary?

MARY. What do you mean?

JOSEPH. Because if you're grieving, or feeling scared, or in pain, you can always talk to me.

MARY *smiles.*

MARY. You know they've actually repealed Section 28 in Scotland?

JOSEPH *holds a nightgown against his body.*

JOSEPH. Are we thinking – soft cotton knit floral short sleeve?

MARY. It's the homosexual lobby.

JOSEPH. Who, me?

MARY. They're opening the floodgates.

JOSEPH (*holding up a second nightgown*). Or is it an 'embroidered sleeveless' kind of night?

MARY *points at the embroidered one.*

Lace trim, excellent choice. Talking of trimming, those toenails need tackling. Ooh, tongue-twister. Try saying that a hundred times. 'Talking of trimming, those toenails need tackling.'

MARY. Don't mock me.

JOSEPH. I'm sorry. In my family, we all do it. I call my brother the Hungry Hippo and he calls me the Sugar Plum Fairy.

MARY. Oh, Jacob, that must be so hard. He shouldn't call you a fairy.

JOSEPH. Why? I give as good as I get. And it's Joseph.

MARY. Pardon?

JOSEPH. My name's Joseph not Jacob.

MARY. And what does your mother think?

Beat.

Doesn't she worry about AIDS?

With a single gesture or look, JOSEPH *shuts this conversation down.*

JOSEPH. I've brought you a midnight feast.

He takes a cake tin from his holdall.

Baked with my own lily-white hands.

MARY. Victoria sponge. (*Opening the lid.*) With fresh raspberries. Thank you.

JOSEPH. Don't tell Edith because I only gave her a scone. I must have a soft spot for you. (*Quietly.*) God knows why.

MARY. What was that?

JOSEPH. It's too late for a bath. Let's go do a flannel wash and I'll tuck you in.

MARY. Oh no, no, please, I need some time in the garden.

JOSEPH. You want to sit here alone in the dark?

MARY. I'm never alone.

Little beat.

JOSEPH. Alright. Twenty minutes.

MARY. Could you please put a slice on a plate?

He obliges.

Tomorrow I will be writing a letter of complaint to Channel Four.

JOSEPH. I'll bring you a stamp, Mary.

Exit JOSEPH.

MARY *is left alone, staring out across the dark garden.*

Beat.

MARY (*talking to God*).
I was supposed to be your instrument of change,
you chose me to do your work on earth
but still I'm holding back the sea, Lord
and some days, I don't know
if I saved a single soul.
I tried my best.
I'm not sure it was good enough.
Was I good enough?

She waits for a response. None comes.

Since Ernest died, I can't quite – hear you – like I used to.
This reminds me of our meadow.
More manicured of course – no fantail pigeons –
but the stars shine the same
and, in my mind's eye,
I can still see those protesters
like a scruffy horizon
right there, within walking distance
yet I can't reach them, Lord.
The bearded man in the tiny waistcoat,
hard-faced women in a great big line,
the floppy-haired boy in the stripy shirt,
all wishing me dead
like naughty children locked out of the house
(*Shivering.*) in the cold.
It's alright, they can't get at me.

Demons with white eyes, staring
across my English meadow.
(*Slapping herself in the face*.)
Quiet Time.

There's a boy.
There's a boy.
There's a boy, he's crossed over, a boy is in our meadow.
Henry? Wait, it's a tree – no, it's a man,
his hair's blowing in his face, he's approaching.
Like a sleepwalker moving through a mist.
Robert.
I can't. You know I can't. Please don't come any closer.
Unless…
You've waited all this time? Oh my love.
Your face is… different.
You're not Robert.
Are you the devil,
come to take me to the dark fire?
Piercing my skin till I'm nothing but…

A great light shines.

Light.

Her relief is immense.

Hello.
You gave me a bit of a shock there.

JESUS *is wearing a white 'Glad to be Gay' T-shirt
and a crown of thorns.*

GAY JESUS. Christ loves everyone, body, soul and spirit, even her. Yes, members of the jury, *even* Mary Whitehouse has the opportunity, has the hope of salvation.

MARY. Lord? My Lord?

GAY JESUS (*quietly*). Would you like to see my wounds?

MARY. Sorry?

GAY JESUS (*quietly*). Would you like to see my wounds?

MARY. I beg your pardon?

GAY JESUS. Would you like to see my wounds?

She tries.
She can't.

MARY. No! No! Absolutely not!

The curtains close slowly.

The End.

NOTTINGHAM PLAYHOUSE

Nottingham Playhouse is dedicated to making bold and thrilling world-class theatre, proudly made in Nottingham. It is joint winner of The Stage Awards' Theatre of the Year 2025.

Nottingham Playhouse is a registered charity, and one of the country's leading producing theatres, renowned for creating ambitious and diverse productions, many of which have toured the UK and transferred to the West End and Broadway.

James Graham's world premiere of *Punch*, based on Jacob Dunne's book *Right from Wrong* and directed by Nottingham Playhouse Artistic Director Adam Penford, transferred to the Young Vic in March 2025. The production will transfer simultaneously to the West End and Broadway in autumn 2025. The critically acclaimed, sell-out five-star production received standing ovations every night and unprecedented audience feedback. James Graham was awarded the Kevin Pakenham Award (Longford Trust) for *Punch*, and David Shields won the Best Performance in a Play (UK Theatre Awards 2024). The original production of *Punch* at Nottingham Playhouse was sponsored by Nottingham Trent University.

In 2024, Adam Penford directed a brand-new, non-replica production of the smash-hit musical *Dear Evan Hansen*, which went on a ten-month UK-wide tour before heading to Manila and Singapore.

As well as the world premiere of *The Last Stand of Mrs. Mary Whitehouse*, this Autumn 25 sees the UK regional premiere of Tony Award-winning *Eureka Day* by Jonathan Spector.

The theatre's Participation department offers over sixty different programmes which create life-changing experiences for the local community. Nottingham Playhouse is a Theatre of Sanctuary and is committed to being a space where everyone feels they belong.

Nottingham Playhouse nurtures the next generation of theatre-makers through its extensive artist support programme, Amplify, which has over 1000 active members and includes a regular programme of performances through AMPLIFY: SEASONS.

Nottingham Playhouse is committed to continually improving its sustainability standards across productions and its Grade II* listed building and in 2024 received a Carbon Literate Organisation Silver Award.

For more information about Nottingham Playhouse visit **www.nottinghamplayhouse.co.uk**.

www.nickhernbooks.co.uk

@nickhernbooks